Our Play

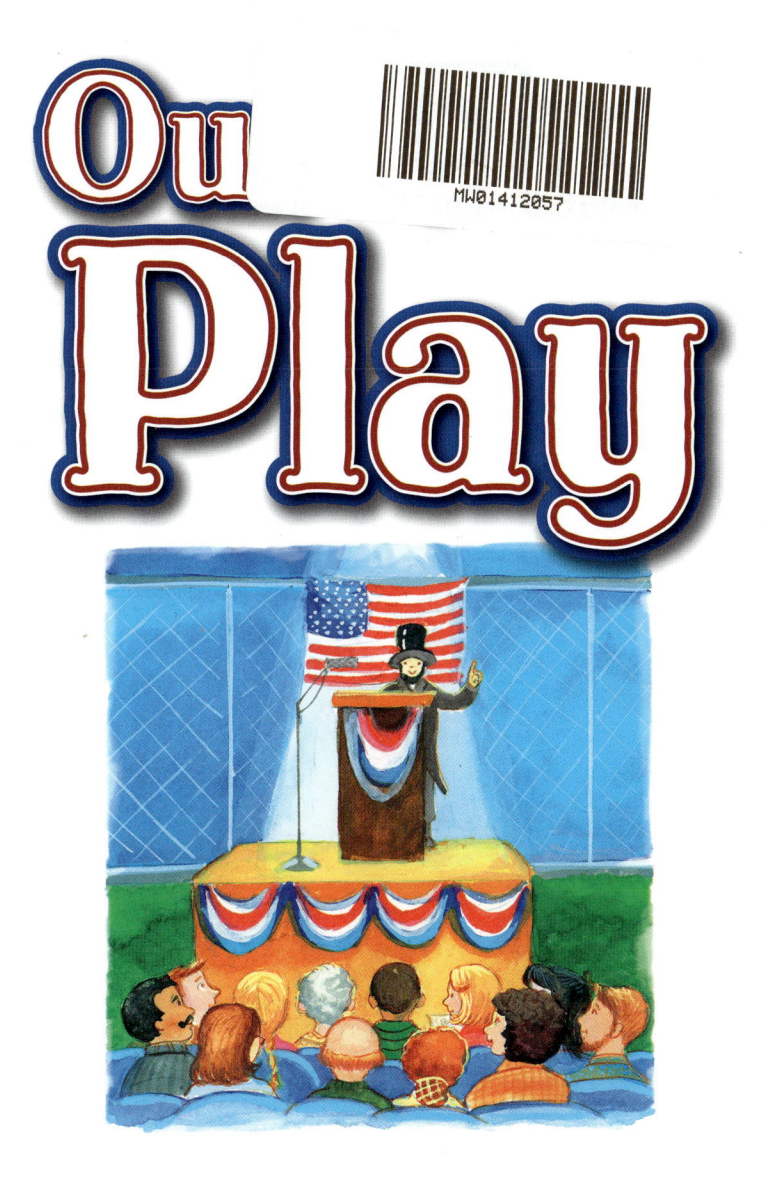

by Gus Gedatus   illustrated by Margeaux Lucas

Scott Foresman
is an imprint of

PEARSON

Glenview, Illinois • Boston, Massachusetts • Mesa, Arizona
Shoreview, Minnesota • Upper Saddle River, New Jersey

Illustrations
Margeaux Lucas

Photographs
Every effort has been made to secure permission and provide appropriate credit for photographic material. The publisher deeply regrets any omission and pledges to correct errors called to its attention in subsequent editions.

Unless otherwise acknowledged, all photographs are the property of Pearson Education, Inc.

8 ©Karl Gerhardt/Corbis

ISBN 13: 978-0-328-39368-8
ISBN 10:   0-328-39368-1

Copyright © Pearson Education, Inc. or its affiliate(s). All Rights Reserved.
Printed in the United States of America. This publication is protected by copyright and permission should be obtained from the publisher prior to any prohibited reproduction, storage in a retrieval system, or transmission in any form or by any means, electronic, mechanical, photocopying, recording, or otherwise. For information regarding permission(s), write to: Pearson School Rights and Permissions, One Lake Street, Upper Saddle River, New Jersey 07458.

Pearson and Scott Foresman are trademarks, in the U.S. and/or other countries, of Pearson Education, Inc. or its affiliate(s).

1 2 3 4 5 6 7 8 9 10 V010 17 16 15 14 13 12 11 10 09 08

We're planning a class play.
It's about Abraham Lincoln.
It will certainly be hard work.

We're planning a class play.
"I'm going to paint a flag!" Lee says.
"What should I do?" Nick asks.
"You're going to be Abraham Lincoln," Mr. Kim says.

We're working on a class play.
"I'll be the worst! People will laugh," says Nick.
"You'll get better," says Mr. Kim.
Nick is better the second time he reads his part.

Our parents come to our class play.
Nick speaks.
He's wearing a beard, a black hat,
and a long coat.

People either clap or cheer at Nick's speech.
Nick feels great.
"I can't wait to be in another play!" he says.

Gettysburg

Read Together

Abraham Lincoln made many great speeches. His most famous might be his speech at Gettysburg. A big Civil War battle took place on a farm field near a town named Gettysburg. The battle lasted three days. President Lincoln gave a speech at the field a few months later. It was a short speech, but it was very special. Lincoln wanted to end the war. He wanted people to remember the battle at Gettysburg. He wanted people to remember the soldiers who had died there.

The field is now a park. People can visit it and remember what happened there.

The field at Gettysburg is now a park.